FALSE
WEIGHT

FALSE WEIGHT

Poems by

Jason David Peterson

Distillate Press

Published by Distillate Press
Copyright © 2021 by Jason David Peterson
All rights reserved
FIRST PRINTING

TYPEFACE: Yu Gothic

Acknowledgement is made to the editors of the following
publications, in which the poems listed first appeared: *Blood
Lotus*, "Baptismal"; *The Fugue*, "Inspiration"; *disClosure,* "How
We Got Here" and "The End of Conversation"; *The Martin Lake
Journal*, "Avenues."

ISBN-13: 978-0-578-88751-7

· CONTENTS ·

Labors

Journeys

Ghosts

A FOREWORD TO THE READER

Forget about the poem for a minute.
There's nothing I can tell you
that isn't already true.

    I can lie though

about the limits of the heart, the size
of blind spaces, how many voices
can fit in a cacophony before
it's less or more of something else.

    I can ask you

to imagine that you don't know
how you feel about a rolling thunder,
the resin of poplar or a blue calf
chipped from marble,

        so you have to

start over—only this time
you don't get to know who you are
exactly, or where a memory
might strike up suddenly yours.

Labors

CONSULTING

Stolen on the whim of a contract,
I'm abandoned in the glow
of cascading schedules
on blue-screen, halls of metal,
popup restaurants awash
in the oils of the tired
and uncomfortable.

Only the outer layers of a traveler
can sustain here, the rest of us
throwing anchor lines home
—even airborne and restrained
in knee-tight vinyl seats
rationalizing a floor of clouds,
there is a trail behind me

so I never fully locate.
Late night check-ins,
vending-machine breakfasts
—I take in fractions
of booming cityscapes
from the windows
of hotel rooms and wait

for the minutes between meetings
when the smell of rain by chance
wanders through a sterile lobby
and permeates, or the walk

across a rural car rental center
—a brief, tactile encounter
with shrubs and grasses, hills and flow,
a little red fox by the curb.

NOTHING POEM

We notice a leaf, for example
—some subtle thing,
its shape or trajectory
briefly surprising.

And we do the math:
is it miraculous,
mistaken, incidental?
Then the numbers go,

unfastened in
a boundless cosmos.
We accept a standard
because we have to

move on—either everything
is a living miracle
or a dead one.
The matter's settled.

So why does that moment still speak
like a coal in the mind's breezeway
—black, orange, black
and burst a wave of yellow?

Like the boy who pulls a stick
from the mud, waving it high
and regal—so much desire
to find a thing special.

GOOD MORNING

You can only say it to
a certain number of people
before it sounds like a parting,
or an *excuse me for being
in the same spot*,
or a *sorry you're not
a priority*—and I feel bad
because what I mean is
we're all going to mutter
things that don't matter
until one day we're bleeding
in or out of somewhere
and I may or may not care
how good a person you were
or which of us goes first—
but I want to recognize
that we clearly both tried
to be all the tiresome things
a person has to be
to stay healthy and clean
and unincarcerated
and respectful of all
the incomprehensible
needs of those around us,
just to keep them
from feeling terrible
and I want to thank you for that
before one of our awkward,
rubbery bodies fails
and the last of our likeness
decays below the surface.

INSPIRATION

The garden is pocked
with migrant catalpas.
Boyish bean sprouts
curve their heads back
to ground, little green
horseshoes of concession.
A bit of remorseless
inter-floral oppression.

I get this.
There's a distinct smell
to a fresh plot,
an open position
—something satiating
about making space
and filling it.

The mushrooms know.
They rise and dawn
their milky sombreros,
make a happy mess
of the measured rows.

I could weed, sailing
a decision. Instead
I water everything,
dress them in trestle
and stomp full ritual
around the perimeter,
chanting all to war.

A well-groomed garden
is an ending spoiled. This
slow game of strangles,
on the other hand,
makes for good soil.

WORKING ON CARS

Fool yourself
once in a while—
it's important.

I say this to the neighbor's dog
who is loose and tracking oil
around my garage while his owner
rolls divorce papers
into a coffee canister.

I say this to the dog
so it won't hit too directly
in the gut of a man who's emptied
but linger more like a work song,
coming in sideways
with the rhythm of a tool in hand.

    And I don't say it lightly; it's impossible
    to know what another goes through—

but having taken half my engine apart
with the assumption
that I could find what's broken

and looking at this pile of bolts
and carefully curved metals
that may never go back together

    —I'm beginning to.

WHEN YOU STOP LOVING YOUR JOB

If it's a sound, it's subtle,
hanging like an icicle
from the corner of the roof
—a soft snapping from above
and this fragile thing that once
connected you   angles loose
and heavy in your glove.

And what then?
Toss it to the snow and weep,
break it into shards   faking
some show of control,
ply it to your tongue to feel
more exactly the nature
of what happened?

In the stale, crashing brown
of your eyes when it dawned,
I saw your life being measured
—the ice melting, scales
tipping, your hands   empty
for the first time in years.

WAITING

—is a sword of a word;
is the fetus healthy
will you get the job
or you'll understand
when you're older

but you never are
and facts unsheathed
are no less sharp
so get to it—kill time

before others catch on
before you even know
what's *waiting for*
or *having done*
or *filling in*

or why it ends
with a sword, either way
the word of a ghost;
the thought of yourself
incomplete.

THE NAMELESS MOST-OF-IT

A career is a false friend.
It's strapping on the rope
and harness, scaling the mountain
one grueling lunge at a time
while never actually connecting
—and what's amazing is
you can do this for decades
fueled only by your own surprise
that you're somehow surviving.

Meanwhile others still at base camp
look up, wondering how you're doing it
and if for a second they should want to
—then returning to their lives
far more filled than yours with passion
and the people who have time
to be around them.

AVENUES

It's been ages
since we drank on the swings
while your father's ghost
packed your head with black
powder and pointed you north.

I want to believe I saw the change
taking place—how a broken family
can fix something the wrong way
and forever, how a set of tools can rust
until everything's a hammer—

but mostly, I saw my own failures
painted on your shoes
and the dim glow of purpose
barely pulsing from your chest
like a firefly.

And what I tried to ask without words:
if you couldn't manage it
—that old American Dream
blazing down on us from the past—

what chance was there
for a shadow like me not to shrink
from the same heavy light
and harden like clay?

QUAKE AND SETTLE

I want to say I understand—
your hands shake at the mention,
your clothed or unclothed body
is a prison—I can't
and there's no right way to imagine.

Your uncontrolled movements
find a way to scream it—
what you couldn't have prevented,
wasn't yours to prevent, maybe
if you were something more
than human, or had always been
impossibly, the person you wish
you had wanted to be—

but that's not prevention,
just thieves in you competing
for the lesser loss
while you are quietly robbed
from outside. Forgive me

all this ignorance, I want to help
—but tell me if you can
in fists or blinks or moans
what I should be building, or
tearing something down for.

THE END OF CONVERSATION

Anyone can scream.
They're doing it in rounds
—overworked throats
and played-out phrases
decoupage our city
in pith and spittle,
so how can I tell you
of outrage? A whisper
carefully delayed,
a currency in flames,
an act of kindness?

There's no wrong answer
but we all still lose, gasping
in the crowded air.

If I were dying now
of that very violence,
it would end me faster
having to explain.
So I lie in silence,
wave my arms
making logic angels
in the massacre
of words, and wait
for a new sound
to articulate.

AUTHORS

Those stars to your right
had no audience,
a vast storeroom of cut footage,
until someone penned a coordinate
—how strong was their love
for the inanimate.

You have to be impossible
to swallow a universe,
fold a tiny version of all of it
inside you—and we are,
we're allowed to.

But space itself should fill
with our sincere and selfless pleas,
the kind that speak through the drift
and arrangement of constellations.

Each of those blips by a mix of forces
burst to life at some point,
may well be ash by now.

Journeys

HALLEY

I rode the bus in quiet awe
with her best friend's little brother
who made up stories of her
to impress me. We both chose
to believe them, as if
playing out a ritual
that could make the heart bow.

I knew of the comet then—
how the fiery body uncontrollable
just hurls out of view, trailing beauty
and you want to see it land
despite the impact
but there's nothing you can do.

LITTERED

No one makes a clean run of life.
We're interactions, like soda cans
our parents open—freshness
slowly depleted, we cave
to the shape of the grip,
then tossed, maybe out a window
of the family vehicle, maybe
into the raucous valley of lanes.

I'm talking about a lifetime
of pings and dents and bangs
—the only kind. And the wounds
make sense; the timing is right,
the wild trajectories seem
precise to pedestrians
on the walk bridge who point
and say "look at that one go."

SYMPATHY

I can ramble
about broken hearts
and failing bodies, rail with you
against old gods and abusive policies,
describe with you a pain so elaborate
even death can't figure it out.

But you are your own grab bag
of nerves and dreams and harmonies.
You have to decide of things their value
and if life is a shell you come out of
or grow into. And if you need me

to be silent while you do;
if there's nothing I can say
because our wounds don't match,
well——

HOW WE GOT HERE

We ate everything in the house.
The yard picked clean—
left not what any
starving memory
could hold out for.
We ate our anger
and soon our love
and the patience of others.
We ate our hunger and moaned
as it grew heavier inside us.
We ate the world raw
and the bitter green
and salty blue and endless
black on black went down
in a flush of burn and clay.
We ate the future
before it limped away.
We ate the rules
of all of this, and now
it has no meaning.
As if nothing was ever
made or eaten—
an infinite nothingness
that won't digest, and so
there is only us.

MOON

She draws out her goodbye
millimeters over millions of years,
straining to escape orbit.
It's not a factor of time, if ever;
belief is a current event.
Though her looking-back gaze
is a fix of sorrow, a courage wells
—her heart already in the vast.

Correction: there are no tropes
of love or loss to arch on.
She is genderless, does not
think ~~herself~~ itself pressed
in a mold of roles or patterns.
It is without mate,
sans appetite, a stone.
A presence only accustomed
by tho light of a giant death
occurring all this time.

UNDER THE OCEAN

It isn't breath-taking
nor the vast jungle of life
promised in documentaries.
Everything just blue.

The coral shy and delicate.
The only shark a small, soft article
fled to cower from the shadow
of our submarine.
And pale schools of fish, lulled
by their own wavering.

I want to care about all of this
—a new world revealed to me,
but I keep looking back
to the Higgins boat, sunk
and half covered in sand.
Its bow ramp leaning out,
still delivering ghosts
in a hail of retired bullets.

The starfish are also at war,
prey for crabs or manta rays
but I don't feel that,
the way I don't fear
a sudden breach or the water
rushing to undo me—
I know where I stand
with these. My wilderness
is the man in the next seat.

ALL ABOARD

Walking seven decks, rail and salt
in circles—a sturdy voice floats
on the ship's radio. I am a captive
in his narrative. He is a captain,
a priest, a transient
across a world of islands
and I know how it happens:
year after year of disintegration,
one day you go and there's nothing
coming home to. You take this role
no one else would, and you
tack up walls around the sky
you've fallen into, hang a door,
have a guest, keep it cool.
We have the same look in our skin—
ages and poison and raging freedom.
The endless horizon does not gain on us
until it suddenly, utterly does.

THE DEAD SEA

Somehow we made it in
at midnight—only
the lights of Jordan
reflecting in the distance;
songs from a cell phone
under sand-swept canvas
and pole, bringing language
back to us; unpacked
wine of Jerusalem
blessing our courage.

After missile strikes at port,
wall on wall of concrete,
wire and rifled silhouettes,
we measured trust
in the length of silences
and daring stretches
of uncovered skin.
We let the salt burn
up to our knees
for a chance to feel
the wash of history
condensed.

I AM AGING, I KNOW

—because the sun stopped setting
the way a wheel at the right speed
feigns not to move. This blood
forced up and through the body
only held in me by centrifuge.
These words so slow to appear
they've broken the other side
of the sound barrier

and

as that virile cloud of meaning
sucks back into nothing,
I can't protect my knowing
from redactions and asterisks
—my second shift begins:
the will to wilt gracefully, the miss
of the miss-ion, the syllabic inversion
of en-list to list-en.

GAMBLE

What excuse will be made for us
sitting again across this table,
prying each other open at the chest?
Every joy its weight in anguish
—the lives we've built contain us.

So what of the break and jump,
the flee and tangle?
The first embrace, of course
but the ones that follow;
unfestooned and normal,
exhausting—

could we survive
the end of wanting?

VOW

I don't drink from words the way I used to,
I can't sustain on a syllable of any density.
I can't pull a name from a river to save its drowning

but I'm replenished by watching the attempt
—the intention of yours to allow a sound
to love another sound in a manner we can't.

And knowing we're as close to the filling
as an empty thing can be—that the shape
of empty is the warrant of being, you gift me
and you gift me again.

FLIGHT

You and I do not listen
to the engines plowing
this hull across the sky.
We feel them—
the lift and the drag
fighting each other
to bring us there
and to prove such a thing
naïve and clumsy,
risen.

Ghosts

CEMETERY KIDS

I can tell you where people go
when a secret is the only
breathable space.

I used to build those places, carve them
from the surface of things
—this is all it takes:

An invisible circle
that becomes real
when you want to be in it.

A mission without reason
where life erupts
from the doing of it.

A wonder stronger than fear
that comes by knowing—we are each
a part of what happens here.

BURYING THE DOG

You brought me to the dig
fresh with the parts of body
that liquefy in time.
You had me shovel
sand over a blank stare,
tender ears bending back.

Cruel, but it made sense
offering her to root
the way water cycles to sky.

Towering maple above
tapped through that year
to muted jars of gold
I couldn't pour
as cake upon cake
cooled slowly on the plate.

CABIN

Wet on wood water,
pale pan of sun,
fly foam droolings,
long blonde lawns,
you're here now

or ten years gone,
returning intangible
—hum of idle meadows.
I hold your never-hand
in numbness contented
and time and time recall it:

the prickly sticky things
we shared, the overtures
we rolled in, the green
preponderant; each
lazy drifting moment
now momentous, yet

all of this—the ghost
and pre-ghost, the layered
haze phases—irreconcilable.
They talk and it's not you.
Same is not the same,
but it's enough.

DEMONS

You used to break quietly
from our childhood sleepovers
and spin the plastic eyes
of all your dolls and animals
facing up. In the morning
we let ourselves believe
something terrible
had claimed the attic
and that was all it took

to interpret sounds, shiver
at the base of the ladder, beg
for stories of the souvenirs
stored above—we didn't know
the entrance never closed for you,
nor the torn wedding dress
you claimed to see floating there
was more than a phantom.

We couldn't imagine a time
when your father wasn't calm
in his robe and pipe, or picture him
heading home from weeks on the road,
your mother crying on the phone,
you hiding among the toys
in your room, praying to something
that refused to love.

POSSESSION

When I first knew my body
was not boundary enough
you held my hands
frozen in the taking
and pushed back
as the walls rocked me.

Imagine a feeling that isn't yours
—an osmosis of intensity,
a dark weight accumulated
in fractions and rounding up
to something you don't recognize
like a mist settling
in the wool of your gravity
that tells you by its hang
where your limbs
should be, but aren't
—a sickness of the self
that, by the time you notice,
belongs to someone else.

When I first knew my body
could be borrowed
you told me to stay
and I watched you say it
from every corner of the room.

NORMALIZING

The woman at the crosswalk
pushes harder on the button
believing some change
should have taken—
all is red.

There are no vehicles.
A yawning moon rolls
up the side of the building.
Two loitering boys disappear,
chasing off a sense of public.

Six pounds of caramel
weigh in the handbag
she refuses to rest—
her shoulder separates,
slides to the curb.

Her other hand, violently striking
crushes in like rhubarb.
She is married to the button.
The lights are moving away,
the poem cannot help.

The street is a river of tar.
Horizon once steep
skews and wanes in tow,
her long name pooling under—
a spring of words we can't know.

MISSING PERSON

Sirens bray down
the Smokehill Scenic;
floater in the swamp today
—muddy magic.
Terrible place to hide
a body, bog trees advise,
lean so far to the answer
they come right out
and say it—this
was one of yours.
I give her back.

EXPLANATIONS

I hear her walk the stairs
just after dinner—those nights
rare with ease, crickets quieted,
humidity settling in on the wood.
I'd come to think she died here.

I don't picture an ivory nightgown,
bare feet or hair pinned for slumber.
I don't imagine a face in any range
of raised to sunken, only
the looping sound of a false weight,
consecutive to a break at the bottom.

I recall our old television—
tape paused and forgotten,
screen burned with the image of a sailor
so that all programs appeared
the dream of a drowned man.

Then also the well-walked dog,
abandoned when his boy
joined the bone tour, who
for years and years after
walked the same park on his own.

There are so many afterlives
packed like clouds in our truth,
we're teased with haunting.
But what hell would hold us
agape with transcendence
only to circle back around?

I hear her walk the stairs
and I hope she is genderless,
bodiless, a pattern without name
—still I ask it of her, night and again
until neither of us could know
whose routine we're in.

FARM HOUSE

The county road lays to miles
of dried mud and crumbled
castles of tar. August sun
has boiled the colors from the sky
and dressed them in glitter,
parading the horizon.

I pull in to a high bank
of prairie green and the chafed
staccato of grasshopper legs
nearly sparking up a fire.

The house is where I left it
twenty years ago—hungover
lengths of stud and age-worn siding,
stale red carcass of arches,
a ghost of a place.

Except the ghost is always bigger
than the building,
pushing around the weight
of its endlessness,
crying out for a time
when it could risk something.

I think of everyone who'd lived here—
thick hands that brought it to shape,
old hands that braced its walls for storm,
rebel hands who'd made a camp of it
crushing bottles and cursing their fickle hearts

—and I wonder
if ghosts board themselves up
inside other ghosts, waiting out
the infinite din,
and if I am among them already
stuck in a memory,
driving this road again.

STORM BREAK

Recall how the dog jumped and scuttled
under the table, knocking himself around
and throwing chairs.

And the wind that tore
as the mass of the world spun
counter to a foreign sky.

And the worry you carried
for your daughters (all now married off)
that pulled at the skin of your heart

like the ripe tomatoes
that clung through the torrent,
hanging wet with strain.

Only so much is ours to save, you mourned
as your steeled hands set to work.

    Through the yard, a wall of harsh and slick,
    you stiffly sloshed and gathered bulbs of red
    until the air exhausted took a breath.

    Sharp arrows of light then broke,
    bending thin columns of shadow on your path
    like a gate to a fullness you couldn't enter.

    But the way you set your pail aside
    and lowered your hood in awe—I have a feeling,
    for a moment, you ventured.

MEDIUMS

When you really understand someone
in a way, you overlap
and though we hadn't spoke of it
I knew that you would know
how to tell me, afterwards
a body was never
all that necessary.

I was convinced
I'd notice something
purposefully out of place,
patterns in dust, chairs
rocking themselves.

I threw everything into a light
that may or may not have been on
when you left.

BAPTISMAL

From below, my canoe's contour
is a rippled cavern on the blind
edge of light, unmetered thuds
of aluminum breaking waves.

Almost clear now
waking from the rush,
images resurface in a flush

—paddle struck and split,
a sudden shift of weight,
slam and tip and red.

—the spinning grip of currents,
drops and dips of a wash
over stubborn rocks
I couldn't hold.

There are mottled shells
embedded in my skin, lungs
braised from sluice and sand,
but something else uncovered:
    a phantom root
that binds me together

—I know
because I feel its snaking pull
when I see your hand, blue-hued
angling through the water.

Take it.
Take it.